T0164338

My Shoshana

My Shoshana

A Father's Journey Through Loss

Rabbi Rafael Grossman
with Anna Olswanger

Eshel Books

Baltimore • Washington

ISBN 978-0-935437-39-3
Library of Congress Control Number: 2011932037

Published by:

ESHEL BOOKS
8600 Foundry Street
Mill Box 2043
Savage, MD 20763
800-953-9929

www.eshelbooks.com

Printed in the United States of America

My Shoshana:
A Father's Journey
Through Loss

Shoshana, I wish you could talk to me and describe to me where you are. I could tell people what you say, even if they answer, "You heard voices. They're not real. You imagined them."

Is there any way you can talk to me?

I want to tell you everything that's happened in the world since you left, the things I wanted you to see and the things I wanted you to have. I want to tell you what you could have done, but I also want you to tell me what you're doing.

Because I believe, with all my heart, you're in that other world. And I want you to tell me what it looks like, if you have friends, if you've seen your grandparents. And I want you to tell me if you've seen any of the heroes or heroines we studied about in the Bible— Abraham, Sarah, Moses, King David.

I want you to tell me: Is it really a good place where you are? But if you tell me that it's a good place, I won't believe that it's better than here, this world where your mother and I made a home for you, and where your brothers and sister are.

I have a photo album in my mind with a million memories of you. I can't forget the day when you were in the first grade and you didn't know I was standing outside the school playground. It was springtime and new leaves covered the trees. You were running and jumping. It was beautiful. It was all that life should be, and I wanted to shout out my joy.

But now, what satisfaction is there in anything called joy if I can't share it with you? I've known the love of a father for his first child, especially his first daughter, and it's something that transcends anything I could have wanted. I never knew it until you were born. And I don't believe that a love so strong could be put in a wooden box in the ground, that it's no more.

When you died, for a while I stopped believing in God. I said, "If there is a God, how could He do this? How could He allow innocence to die? My Shoshana never did anything wrong." I thought death was a punishment for bad things. But what bad things did you ever do? Even when you were little, I never saw you do anything mean to your brothers or your sister. If you were jealous of them, I didn't see it.

Everything you were stands vividly before me now. So you've got to be alive somewhere. If you're not alive, then death really is ugly and bleak. If there is a God, someone like you has to continue living. But if there is a God, you shouldn't have died.

I want to talk to you about that. Have you found out why young people die? It's one of the questions I want you to answer. If you can tell me, then maybe I can tell the thousands of others who ask the same question.

If there is supposed to be death, it should only be for old people who had a chance to live and know joy. You knew some joy, but it wasn't your own. It was what you shared with your family and your classmates. You didn't have a chance to make your own joy— your own marriage, children, career. So I want you to tell me what you've found out about life and death, and what your purpose was in the seventeen years that you lived on this earth.

*T*he week before you started first grade, we had to take you to a child psychologist for an intelligence test. That was the school policy where we lived. The psychologist walked out of his office afterward to talk to your mother and me.

"I've been doing this for thirty years," he said, "and I've never tested a five-year-old with your daughter's logic and sense of responsibility. I asked her what she would do if she were walking by some train tracks and saw a train crash into a car. She said she would run to the nearest house or store and phone an ambulance. Do you know what other children tell me? They say: 'I'll call my mommy. I'll run away. I'll close my eyes.'

"I asked Shoshana if she would call the police.

"'First, you have to take care of the hurt people,' she said."

When the psychologist repeated your words to me, I realized I was hearing my own religious philosophy. I put the preservation of life above all else. I never thought I had taught it to you, but somehow you knew it. Your mind was connected to your heart. You were only five years old, but surely you had as much to give the world as any mathematical prodigy.

And then the psychologist said, "Please be careful with her. A child like this could grow up to be frustrated and disillusioned. I doubt that she will ever be in a school where other children will have her level of understanding. She could end up very lonely."

But we didn't have to be careful

with you. Even though you always had the answer, you sat in the back of the classroom from the day you set foot in school. Your teachers told us you never ran to the front, you were never the first to answer a question, you waited and gave respect to your classmates.

And each day you came home with something new, something exciting to share with your mother and me. You remembered everything. At night, when you talked on the phone with your friends, I heard you explain the homework assignments, but never impatiently. Your friends were crazy about you.

In my lifetime, more than six million Jews died in the Holocaust. But I believe Judaism remained alive so that the world could benefit from its truths and teachings. I saw you as a person who could embody all that. I saw that God had entrusted me with one of His valued possessions, someone who could make the world brighter, who could bring joy to her people.

I never had any doubts about your being a leader. I knew success was inevitable for you, so what I wanted was for you to be a happy, caring person. I wanted someone someday to love you as much as I did, to cherish you, admire you. And I wanted you to have the same blessings I had—the pleasure of your own children.

After you died, I studied about the hereafter in writings and books by the mystics called kabbalists. I wanted to know what they had to say about the next world. I even investigated other religious beliefs, those of the East and the West. Now, after many years, I have to believe in the hereafter because it's the only place I can find you.

I imagine what it's like where you are. I grew up believing in a Garden of Eden with angels ministering to God and serving the righteous, but that's not what I see in my mind now.

I see a garden with flowers and brooks of water. I see day and night, with stars so near I could touch them. I see a bright sun. I see people with smiles. And I see you as a small child, jumping and dancing.

I listen, and sometimes I hear hundreds of voices. They're old and young, and when I hear the young ones, I wonder why they're there, why they look no different than they did before they died.

You look the same, too. In this garden, your dress never changes and your face never shows age. I want to stop you for a moment and say, "Here I am," and I want to watch you run toward me, shouting, "Daddy, Daddy!"

What's it like there? I see you and I see silhouettes of others, but I don't see God. I wonder if He's there.

I remember each day of the summer we spent together in Israel before you died. I've been to Israel dozens of times since then, and each time, I see you there.

I go up to the plaza above the Western Wall and look down at the women's section where I see you praying. And I see you at the Sea of Galilee, in Tiberias, in Tsefat, at the waterfalls of Banias, and on Mt. Carmel. I see you beside the long roads that crisscross Israel.

Do you remember the funny truck we hired in Jerusalem? It had two rows of seats in the cab and two rows of benches in the back. You sat in the cab with the driver and your mother and me.

We sang all the way up to the Golan Heights, then we sang all the way down. We didn't stop singing, and we didn't stop marveling at the little country that you loved passionately.

At Mt. Carmel you told us the story about Elijah and the priests of Baal, at Megiddo you told us about Solomon's Stables, and at Meron you told us about Israel's defeat at the hands of the Romans. You quoted Rabbi Shimon

Bar Yochai: "You will see someday that our children and our children's children will study and live by the Torah."

I still see Israel through your eyes. You were a young girl then, twelve years old. The world was just beginning to unfold before your eyes, and, yet, you were on a first-name basis with everything you saw.

After you died, I knew that if I did certain things, you would be proud of me. As a rabbi, I've chaired many organizations and traveled to many communities throughout the world. But I have to tell you, honor didn't motivate me. Honor, power, money—all those things—lost their meaning after you died. The taste for them has never come back. But I knew you would be proud to say, "Look, that's my daddy." So every time my name appeared in the newspaper, I asked myself, "Did she see it? If she did, is she smiling?"

I wish it were the other way around. I wish I could pick up the newspaper and see your name, read about the things you had accomplished.

I imagine reading *The New York*

Times and seeing that Shoshana Grossman won this award or that award. You might have cured some terrible disease; you said you wanted to become a physician.

But if you had changed your mind and become a teacher, a writer, a social worker, an artist, or anything under the sun, I know your achievements would have been outstanding.

I remember the way you faced your illness. You were prepared to do anything your mother and I asked, including going through painful surgeries and medical procedures. That was a vote of confidence in us on your part and a measure of your faith in God.

I believe that the next world exists. And I believe that you're there. But as much as I want to hear your voice and hear your answers to my questions, I know you can't talk to me. The Torah forbids necromancy. But I do believe that righteous, dead people can intercede on behalf of living loved ones, and I have often felt that the blessings we've enjoyed since you left were because of your prayers. I believe you can communicate with me through feelings.

I'll tell you how I've felt your presence.

Your youngest brother Yehoshua didn't understand what was happening when you died. He kept staring at the door to your room and asking us where you were. He was confused by everyone's behavior.

Your other brother Shamai seemed afraid of being abandoned and kept following your mother and me around.

Your sister Aviva cried endlessly. You were an integral part of all their lives. When you davened, when you did your schoolwork or helped out around the house, you taught them by your example.

But the first product of your teaching was your oldest brother Hillel. At his bar mitzvah, we were still grieving. It was only six months after we lost you. What propelled us to go on was remembering how, before you died, you said you wanted us to celebrate his bar mitzvah. We followed your wishes, and that gave us great pleasure.

I knew you were there that Shabbos. I didn't think that I heard messages from you, and I didn't try to talk to you, but I knew that if we celebrated the way you had wanted, you would be with us.

Hillel's davening and Torah reading were superb. His demeanor, his kindness, his gentleness came through. In rabbinic families like ours, the bar mitzvah offers a Talmudic discourse on Shabbos. Hillel gave the same Talmudic discourse I had given when I became bar mitzvah, and this hemshech, this continuity, comforted me.

I was afraid that sometime during the weekend your mother or I would break down, but we didn't. And I knew that you wouldn't have wanted us to. Many people came—almost all your aunts and uncles and cousins—to spend those three days with us.

We had two parties on Sunday, which was your idea. We had a brunch in the morning for the entire congregation, and a dinner in the evening for close friends and relatives. We had a band, a singer, and dancing. Hillel was happy, and his happiness had much to do with you.

You know that every day we say the prayer that refers to God as the king who loves righteousness and justice. Just a few days after you died, Hillel had came up to me and said, "I don't think I can say that prayer again." When I asked him why, he said, "How could God have allowed Shoshana to die if He's righteous and just?"

But somewhere in his bar mitzvah, Hillel found his faith again. Somehow he saw the other dimension—the dimension we should try to keep in front of us and never lose—that through the sadness and darkness, some light pierces through.

A Jewish boy becoming bar mitzvah is a statement that the thread of Judaism doesn't unravel. To me, it's a statement that, despite the devastation of the Holocaust, we still rejoice in the very things our enemies wanted to destroy. With a bar mitzvah, another young Jew makes the public commitment to practice the mitzvot, to study and adhere to our traditions, to continue the thread of Jewish life. I saw how Hillel, the product of your teaching, shared his enthusiasm and passion for our traditions with everyone at his bar mitzvah.

*L*ess than six months later, we decided that we needed to leave our home in New Jersey—not because we wanted to run away or because we wanted to forget you. We just wanted normalcy, to be part of a community where people weren't forever saying, "We're so sorry for you."

I accepted an offer from a synagogue in Tennessee. I discovered I had chosen a congregation with little future. The neighborhood had changed, and most of the members had moved away. In a sense, it was a blessing because it allowed me to throw myself into the challenge of rebuilding the congregation and letting go of my memories of your death.

During my first few years there, my sermons were rooted in deep pain. The congregation didn't know I spoke from a broken heart. They thought I cried out for all human anguish. And I was sure they didn't want to hear my personal cry. What's the proverb? Laugh, and the whole world laughs with you. Cry, and you cry alone.

But I never tried to conceal my feelings, and at that time, I kept speaking about love, teaching about it, and trying to move people to become more loving because my own love had been seriously wounded.

What do people do with such a wound? If they can, they treat it. But I knew there was no treatment for my wound. I wanted to let it heal, but could I really permit that? One of the greatest fears I had, and this is the same fear I have found in many grieving parents, is the fear of letting go, because letting go implies acceptance.

It implies reconciliation to this terrible thing that I didn't expect to happen but did happen. It implies coming to grips with death—your death—and its consequences.

When we celebrated your brother Shamai's bar mitzvah three years later, we followed what we called, "The Shoshana Plan." The alternative was to say, "How can we possibly rejoice when look what's missing? We're incomplete, we're not finished. We're grieving."

Instead, we celebrated Shamai's bar

mitzvah—even more than we did Hillel's—as our thanksgiving for having had you. We did everything as though you were there and had planned it.

You used to complain that the celebrant got ignored, so we focused on Shamai and his friends throughout all Shabbos. For the parties, we let Shamai choose the music, the musicians, the colors, the decorations, and the invitations. The weekend was entirely what he wanted. And he wanted it to be happy and exciting.

Even though the distance was great, and time had elapsed, I felt your presence at Shamai's bar mitzvah even more than I had at Hillel's. I felt you everywhere, and I didn't want you to see a grieving father.

I wanted you to see what everyone saw—a father who was blessed to see his second son become bar mitzvah, join the ranks of Israel, and accept the responsibilities of Torah.

*D*o you know what happens to most parents like your mother and me? They hide from their child's death and become depressed. I've seen statistics as high as seventy percent for couples who divorce after losing a child. I think they divorce because they want to run away from their loss. I've seen this many times.

Grieving parents join support groups, but they don't say, "We're going to perpetuate the memory of our child and make her life meaningful." If the child died from cancer, for example, or from heart disease, if she was deformed at birth, whatever it was, parents who feel that kind of pain could make a difference in the lives of other children.

After your death, I decided to try to

help others suffering from serious illness. If I could, I led them to the best possible medical care. I made it my business to learn all I could about doctors and hospitals. I wanted to teach people that it's within our capacity to defy death.

I also tried to comfort those who had lost family and friends to serious illness. It's important to commiserate, to listen, to help mourners talk. The halacha is that the mourner should talk about the deceased loved one, so I tried to help people do this. "However you're grieving is all right," I assured them. I wanted to restore their faith and hope, even to share my own questions.

I get calls from all parts of the country, as well as from overseas, about why children die. People from South Africa or Australia think I can open up a box and pull out answers. The truth is, there are no answers. There never will be. Why is there death? Jews believe that God wants humans to live forever, but that humans choose not to. They perpetuate violence; they fail to prevent and cure diseases. And violence and disease kill many young people.

So when I got a call from the father of a four-year-old boy who died in an automobile accident, and the mother of a nineteen-year-old girl who died of leukemia, I never said, "I know how you feel because I feel the same way." No two people can feel the same way. Each of us feels pain, anger, even guilt differently.

And, yes, I feel guilt for what happened to you. Parents who bring children into this world are supposed to protect them. They feel terrible guilt when a child dies. I couldn't prevent your falling ill, but I feel guilty nevertheless.

Do you remember a discussion we once had when you told me I was obsessed with death because all my academic and scholarly interests were related to it? With all the studying, all the thinking, I wasn't prepared for your death. The only way I got through it was with the help of a colleague, a rabbi who visited us frequently and was willing to listen to me and our family.

"Change your scenery and you'll find hope," he said.

The Talmud teaches that a change of place brings a change of fortune, so I followed my colleague's advice. That was when we moved to Tennessee.

Eventually, I realized that the best I could do for other people who had lost a child, even elderly parents who had lost a middle-aged child, was to be their friend, what my colleague had become for me. If each of us could find someone we trusted, someone who didn't make demands, who would listen to us, then we could begin to heal. I'm not grateful for knowing this. I wish I didn't know it because of your death, but regardless of how I came to know it, I now sit with people for hours—and not as a therapist, a counselor, or a clergyman—but as someone who cares, who just wants to understand.

Over the years I've learned that people who try to comfort mourners usually do it the wrong way. They think mourners need to be distracted and turned away from their pain. They couldn't be more wrong. Comfort comes from talking about a loved one, from hearing about her or his special qualities.

Although it's been decades since

you died, I don't stop talking about you. This is the most comforting thing I know. Because in talking about you, a part of you lives. I encourage other people to do the same. I think this is something you would want me to do. And when I do it, I say, "This goes on Shoshana's side of the ledger." It's a mitzvah for you.

*J*udaism recognizes that mourners need to restore their faith. That's why it requires them to go to shul every day for a year to say kaddish, the prayer that affirms faith in God at the very time when faith is nearly impossible.

I find it strange that in Jewish law, a child has to say kaddish for a parent but a parent doesn't have to say kaddish for a child. After you died, I wanted to keep what faith I had, so every day I went to shul and said kaddish for you. I also studied Mishnah in your memory, but found little relief in it.

Then it was Yom Kippur, less than a year after you had died. Someone came up to me on the pulpit to tell me that Anwar Sadat had ordered his army to cross Israel's border. Later, I heard that the Egyptians had penetrated the Bar-Lev Line, the electronic fence in the Sinai desert. They had crossed ravines and military obstacles. They had moved beyond the Sinai and were so close to unprotected Israeli soil that they were within one hour of Tel Aviv. This was nothing like the Six-Day War in 1967. Young soldiers were dying by the hundreds. Israel was losing the war, and I was terrified by what might happen.

Then a congregant told me that his nephew had been killed in the Sinai.

"At least your nephew died for a reason," I said.

The man shook his head. "No one dies for a reason."

I knew he was right. Almost three thousand Israeli soldiers died in that war, and their deaths were as irrational as yours. Each of them died because the rest of us are obsessed with war, power, might—everything but life. No one, especially a young person, dies for a reason, so why does God permit it?

A few weeks later the Israelis captured Egyptian tanks in the Sinai and placed their own soldiers inside. Undetected, they crossed a pontoon bridge over the Suez Canal, encircled the en-

tire Egyptian Third Army, and com-
pelled it to surrender. Israel won the
Yom Kippur War.

"How could Israel have won?" people asked. The Israelis themselves didn't
understand how it had happened. The
Soviets had threatened to enter on the
side of the Arabs, and the Americans
had dragged their feet in giving Israel
the weapons and tanks it needed.

"Only God could have done this,"
I told myself.

Over the years, other miracles,
little ones, restored more of my faith.
One of your baby nieces had a fever

that "ran off the thermometer." We were all afraid she might die, but somehow—from 107 degrees—her temperature returned to normal and she continued to grow into a healthy little girl. I saw other children recover from untreatable illnesses, and each time I could only say, "These are gifts from God."

So now my faith is strong, very strong. But my questions to God are just as strong. I know I have to believe, as Jews have always believed, that I will hear the answers to my questions after the Messiah comes.

For now, I thank God for the miracles He does provide—for the leaves that turn to bright colors in the fall, for the ripples that sweep rivers, for the flow of life through our bodies. And I believe that you're living there in that other world, and that, too, is a miracle. I attribute all that to God.

I considered myself a Freudian before you died. Freud wrote that love is a created object, that the artist, for example, takes a part of herself and places it into a painting, or that the composer takes a part of himself and places it into a symphony. That's how they share their feelings. This is "object love," love with substance.

The Talmud, on the other hand, teaches that when love is dependent on an object or a cause, once the object or cause is gone, the love is gone. After you died, I asked myself every day, "Do I love you?" And the answer was always, "Yes, nothing has changed." So I saw that Freud was wrong. Love is not dependent on an object, and I also saw that love is like faith. It's a gift from God to the person who feels it.

I hunger sometimes for the love I knew when you were a growing adolescent and alive with us. But I also know that once people love each other, the love becomes an entity unto itself. My love for you is indestructible, even though you're living in that other world.

I still go to your grave in New York where we buried you next to your grandfather. I'm sure you know it. I cry, put little rocks on top of your tombstone, pull the weeds, and say the prayers that Jews have always said at gravesides. At home, your mother and I display your photographs. Why not? We still love you. We want to talk about you to others. We always want to remember you.

And now, years after you died, I remember you for all the moments I had with you—the happy and tragic ones. I think about the joys you created in your short life, and I allow my memories of you to stay alive in their own compartment of my soul.

Your siblings often talk about you to their children. Your sister Aviva talks about your love of learning, your passion for the land of Israel and for Torah, and about your special relationship with God. Aviva, Hillel, Shamai, and Yehoshua tell your nieces and nephews how much they love you.

Some people ask me why your mother and I never had another child after you died. The answer is that she and I accepted a truth that many people never come to grips with: There are no replacement children. No child could take your place. Although your brother Shamai is a grown man whose youngest daughter carries your name, she's not you. You lived, you were, and you still are.

So, I believe that in the world to come, when parents will join with their children, and children will join with their parents, grandparents, relatives and friends, I will laugh with you again and sing with you again. In this Garden of Eden with its flowers, brooks of water, and stars so near I could touch them, I will stop you for a moment to say, "Here I am." I will watch you will run toward me, shouting, "Daddy! Daddy!"

And then I will know that God is there.

Glossary

daven. Pray

halacha. Jewish law

Mishnah. Rulings and deliberations of early Talmudic scholars

mitzvah. Good deed. In another context, "commandment."

mitzvot. Commandments

Shabbos. Jewish Sabbath

shul. Synagogue

Talmud. Source of Jewish law

Torah. The first five books of the Hebrew scriptures

Rabbi Rafael Grossman

Rafael Grossman is known throughout the Jewish world as a champion of centrist Orthodoxy and Zionism. The descendant of several generations of rabbis, he is past president of the Beth Din of America and the Rabbinical Council of America.

Rabbi Grossman is Senior Rabbi Emeritus of Baron Hirsch Congregation in Memphis, Tennessee, one of the largest Modern Orthodox congregations in America. His Web site is *www.rafaelgrossman.com.*

Anna Olswanger

Anna Olswanger is a literary agent with Liza Dawson Associates in New York, and the author of *Shlemiel Crooks*, a Sydney Taylor Honor Book and PJ Library Book. Ms. Olswanger has been a student of Rabbi Grossman's since 1977. Her Web site is *www.olswanger.com*.